The Country Houses and Castles of Royal Deeside

Volume One: Lower Deeside

W. Stewart Wilson

Woodlands House

Early maps indicate that Woodlands House, north of Cults, and an adjoining quarry to the south west, were in existence from at least 1860. At that time the surrounding lands remained undeveloped. The house was given individuality by a corner drum tower with a decorative ironwork circlet. The extensive grounds and gardens were developed in the early part of the 20th century. The estate was purchased by Aberdeen Corporation in May 1947. Initially they used it as a home for 50 mentally handicapped children, opening in 1948 after having transferred to the National Health Service. It was the only institution of its type in the north east and was extended in 1952, but declared surplus to requirements in 2003 when plans were considered by Aberdeen City Council to make the land available for new housing and convert the house into flats.

Text © W. Stewart Wilson, 2020.
First published in the United Kingdom, 2020,
reprinted 2021, 2023,
by Stenlake Publishing Ltd.,
54-58 Mill Square,
Catrine, Ayrshire,
KA5 6RD

Telephone: 01290 551122
www.stenlake.co.uk

ISBN 9781840338843

Printed by Blissetts,
Unit 1, Shield Drive,
West Cross Industrial Park,
Brentford, TW8 9EX

The publishers regret that they cannot supply copies of any pictures featured in this book.

Acknowledgements

I should like to thank all those who have given of their local knowledge including Gordon Casely, Chis Engel, Jim Henderson, Professor David Walker and David W. Walker.

Introduction

The last ice caps finally disappeared from Deeside about 10,000 years ago and the earliest inhabitants came soon after. Traces of these early settlers were found near Banchory in 1905 when pygmy flints were found in a field near Birkwood. These early flint implements may well date from 8500 BC. By 5500 BC the land was being farmed and interesting excavations of the late 1970s at Balbridie 3 miles east of Banchory found traces of a remarkable timber-framed building of quite an extraordinary size. An interesting relic of probably 4000 BC is the burial cairn which can be seen on the north side of Cairn Road in Bieldside. The Romans came to Deeside, first in 83 A.D. at the battle of Mons Graupius, and later around 210 AD when the Roman Emperor Septimius Severus forded the river at Tilbouries west of Culter and on the high ground on the north bank built, Normandykes, a great marching camp.

It was the coming of the new turnpike road replacing the old Deeside road, on the north side of the Dee that brought a large influx of people to the area. It had reached Banchory by 1802 and was completed as far as Braemar by 1857, The first tourist guide by James Brown was published in 1831 *A Guide to the Highlands of Deeside*. It was only in 1869, three years after his death, that it was discovered that the author was Joseph Robertson who had written the guide at the age of 21 whilst on holiday in Ballater. In his book he was less than generous in his opinion that the tourist was beginning to affect the area and was about to be 'desolated by cockneys and other horrid reptiles'.

With the arrival of Queen Victoria to Balmoral all that was to change. By 1868 when Queen Victoria wrote about her 'dear Paradise' in her *Journal of our Life in the Highlands* and told the world about its delights, the tourists had arrived. The railway had opened up the area – the line of the Deeside Railway from Aberdeen reached Banchory in September 1853 and was subsequently extended to Aboyne in December 1859 and to Ballater in October 1866. Thus the tourist intrigued by the royal association was able to gain entry to the valley from the coast. Ease of transport to Aberdeen by railway was also desired by those living south of the river and bridges were built to allow access to stations where previously ferries and fords had been the only means of crossing the Dee.

When Robert Louis Stevenson was on holiday in Braemar in 1881 he complimented the Queen on her choice of Balmoral as her summer residence when he wrote in a letter to a friend – 'the Queen knows a thing or two – she has picked out the finest habitable spot in Britain'.

With the discovery of oil in the North Sea in the early 1970s, Deeside saw a rapid expansion of house building and it became one of the most desirable places to set up home in the north east. It is unfortunate that the decision to close the railway was taken in the sixties – today it might have provided a most useful and convenient link to the city. However, the track has been preserved and developed as a popular walkway and cycle track.

This book shares the history of some of the many country houses and castles of Lower Deeside and is the companion volume to the one for Upper Deeside. It does not give the reader their detailed architecture. This can be explored in other books but especially:

Deeside and the Mearns – an illustrated Architectural Guide by Jane Geddes published in 2001.
Aberdeen – an illiustrated Architectural Guide by W. A. Brogden published in 2012.
Aberdeenshire: South and Aberdeen by Joseph Sharples, David Walker and Matthew Woodworth published in 2015.

Woodbank

By the beginning of the 19th century, the power and influence of the Menzies family, who were Catholic and Jacobite, was in decline and their stone-built tower house at Pitfodels was in ruins. In 1805 John Menzies put the lands of Pitfodels up for sale which led to villas being built on the north side of the Deeside Road between Mannofield and Cults. These villas had commanding views across the valley of the Dee. Woodbank was one of the most ambitious and dates from 1848 with additions in 1881. It had a beautiful circular walled garden, along with some magnificent Victorian greenhousesand even had a small 9 hole golf course! The house was owned until 1980 by the Reid family who had an accountancy business in Aberdeen. Walter Alexander Reid sold the house in 1980. Today it is owned by the Shell Pension Fund and is used as a hotel, conference and leisure facility.

Countesswells House

Countesswells House is situated at the northern edge of Cults. In 1750 Alexander Livingstone, a merchant in Aberdeen, became Lord Provost, and purchased from the Irvines of Murtle the estate of Cults which included Countesswells. He added to an existing house dating from 1741, described at the time as 'a new house of three storeys'. In 1752, along with business partners, he set up the Porthill linen company in Aberdeen which was to prove unsuccessful. About eleven years later the company ceased business. Livingstone sold off his whole belongings – including all his property – and with the proceeds satisfied the creditors, who, to mark their appreciation of his conduct, presented him with a handsome dinner service with his arms painted upon them, perhaps a reminder of his days at Countesswells. The estate was sold in 1763 for £10,500 to George Chalmers and eleven years later to William Durward who carried out many improvements to the land and the house.

Bieldside House

It was the coming of the new turnpike road in 1798, replacing the old Deeside road on the north side of the Dee, and the opening in 1853 of the Deeside Railway as far as Banchory that brought a large influx of people to the area. In 1886 the *Aberdeen Journal* reported 'Picturesque Deeside begins at Cults; nowhere is the Aberdonian craze for building houses – fine houses too – more forcible illustrated'. One house, Bieldside House, however, predates this. The lowest part of the house was built in the early part of the 19th century. George Watt, a partner in the Brown and Watt, architects in Aberdeen, added to the house in 1903 for his own use. The house was well suited for easy access to the Deeside railway – there were two stations, one at West Cults, opened in 1894 and the other in 1897 at Bieldside, which made for easy transport to Aberdeen. The railway is long gone but Bieldside remains a very desirable place to live. In a recent newspaper report it was claimed that Bieldside is one of the wealthiest areas in Scotland and is home to the most millionaires per postcode outside London.

Murtle House

In 1163 the barony of Murtle was granted by Malcolm IV to the Bishop of Aberdeen. The lands of Murtle had many owners over the next 600 years and by 1800 they were in the possession of John Gordon. He died in 1821 and his gravestone has the inscription 'John Gordon of Murtle Esq, merchant, Aberdeen, who lived respected and died regretted at the age of 62 having bequeathed his fortunes for charitable purposes'. The lands were purchased from his executors by John Thurburn who had amassed a fortune abroad. Murtle gets its name from the Gaelic *mor-tulach* meaning 'great knoll' and it is on that knoll that in 1823 he built his house to the design of the architect Archibald Simpson. Simpson's work made full use of the special qualities of granite and his talents as a designer and town planner were put to good use in many buildings in Aberdeen. John Thurburn spent large sums in beautifying the grounds and improving the property, which became one of the most choice residences on Deeside. In 1944 the estate was sold and now forms part of the Camphill Rudolf Steiner Schools.

Beaconhill

The coming of the railway to Deeside created an opportunity to live out of the city but have easy access to it. The station at Murtle was opened in 1853 with a journey time to Aberdeen of less than twenty minutes. Although the line did not close until 1966, stations which were not profitable and not able to maintain staff had an earlier fate. Murtle closed in 1937 when the railway could no longer compete with bus travel and the much increased use of the private car. David Montagu Alexander Chalmers, the last member of the Chalmers family to work for the *Aberdeen Journal*, lived at Beaconhill a Victorian granite built house. He was an advocate and the great-great grandson of the founder James Chalmers. He never married and died in 1929. The house was bought by W. L. Cook, a member of the family who owned John S. Cook, ship brokers in Aberdeen. He in turn sold it to Captain John S. Allan, a Director of Alex Pirie and Sons Ltd., paper manufacturers.

Binghill

Binghill House, overlooking Milltimber, was built around 1840. The *New Statistical Account* compiled in that year states that the proprietor Colonel Alexander Kyle 'built a neat and substantial country seat'. He had bought the estate in 1808 and it remained in the family's possession until 1885 when it was sold to Martin Lindsay Hadden. Milltimber originally had only been a small cluster of houses but with the coming of the railway it grew dramatically as the land between the station and Binghill House was redeveloped. The new owner made substantial additions to the house and in 1900 a billiard room and other accommodation was added on a single storey extension at the west end of the house. Before the First World War the house was owned by William Mackinnon whose son Captain Roy Mackinnon died in 1921, aged 29, as a result of a gunshot wound he suffered in France in 1918. Even though his death was a direct result of the war, his name was not added to the Scottish National War Memorial at Edinburgh Castle until 2013.

Edgehill

Edgehill, standing on a fine elevated site with a southern exposure, was built by John Webster, Lord Provost of Aberdeen for three years from 1856 and elected member of Parliament for Aberdeen in 1880. He also took a keen interest in the University of Aberdeen and for 30 years acted as assessor to the Lord Rector. The house was sold to Thomas Jaffrey sometime after 1920. His wife was a keen gardener and the gardens were much admired. Thomas Jaffrey had joined the North of Scotland Bank in 1877 and in 1892 was appointed actuary of the Aberdeen Savings Bank, a post he held for 37 years. After his retirement he served as the bank's consulting actuary until his death in 1953. He had many achievements and served the community in many ways – he was Lord Rector's Assessor in the Court of the University of Aberdeen from 1924 to 1937, chairman of the Aberdeen Art Gallery Committee and chaired the Aberdeen branch of the Royal Horticultural Society. He was knighted in the 1920 New Year Honours and created a Baronet in 1931. On 27th April 1946 Winston Churchill received the Freedom of the City of Aberdeen and accompanied by his wife Clementine, he visited Edgehill where he planted a tree. The house was sold in the mid 1950s and subsequently demolished to make way for a new house on the site.

Ardbeck

In 1872 John Walker, an advocate in Aberdeen, acquired more than 10 acres of land at Milltimber where he built his mansion house Ardbeck. The house is now quite close to the Aberdeen Western Peripheral Route opened in late 2018. When the road was under construction an unexpected discovery was the presence of much earlier activity at Milltimber, likely dating from around 83 AD. Ninety bread ovens were uncovered, which were probably used by the Roman army at a time of invasion led by the Roman general, Agricola. However, no evidence of an associated camp was found. John Walker was followed as owner by Margaret Douglas Chalmers, the only daughter of Charles Walker, grandson of James Chalmers the founder of the *Aberdeen Journal* in 1848. She was born in 1832, never married and died at Ardbeck in January 1927 aged 94. Lachlan Mackinnon, an Aberdeen advocate, bought the house and when he died in 1948 he was succeeded by his son of the same name. Soon after he exchanged Ardbeck for Fairhill, also in Milltimber. The new owner was Thomas Walker, a trawler owner, who died in October 1953.

Culter House

Early in the 13th century extensive lands of Culter along both banks of the river formed part of the possessions of the powerful Durward family – the hereditary door-wards to the kings of Scotland. In 1247 lands on the north bank were given to Robert Wauchope by Alexander II. A chapel dedicated to St. Peter had already been built there by the Durwards. By the end of that century the lands had passed to the Cumin family through marriage to the granddaughter of Robert Wauchope. The 'Ha' Hoose' of the Cumins was built circa 1650 a little to the north east of what we now call Peterculter and replaced an earlier house on the same site. In 1721 Sir Alexander Cumin had the house remodelled by Alexander Jaffrey of Kingswells. Above the entrance on the south front is their coat of arms – two ostrich supporters bearing the family shield with its three sheaves of corn and the motto 'Courage'. The Cumin family appear to have been both extravagant and eccentric – one laird had his horse shod with silver shoes when he attended the marriage of Mary, Queen of Scots and the 15th laird in 1729 was persuaded by a dream of his wife to visit the Cherokee Indians in America and came back as their chief and lawgiver! The laird by this time was bankrupt and the estate had been acquired by the lawyer Patrick Duff. It was again sold, in 1908, to Theodore Crombie of Grandholm, but in 1910 the house was badly damaged by fire. During the renovations two wings were added. Dr. A. Marshall Mackenzie, a notable Aberdeen architect, purchased the house and grounds in 1924 and in 1938 it became the home of Dr. Theodore Watt. In 1946 St. Margaret's School for Girls acquired the property and used it as a house for their boarders for the next 40 years.

Banchory House

The lands of Banchory-Devenick were granted in 1244 by Alexander II to the abbots of Arbroath. In the grounds of Banchory House is preserved the stronghold of Alan Durward of Coull dating from around 1256. Over the next 500 years Banchory-Devenick was owned by many families until 1743 when it was sold to Alexander Thomson an advocate in Aberdeen. He was succeeded by his nephew Andrew whose grandson Alexander inherited the property in 1806. In 1839 he commissioned the Aberdeen architect John Smith, known as 'Tudor Johnny', to build the present house, possibly built on the foundations of a former house dating from 1621. Within the grounds there is a monument in commemoration of Prince Albert's visit to the house on 14th September 1859. The Prince was attending the meeting of the British Association for the Advancement of Science being held in the Music Hall in Aberdeen built especially for the event, as a development of the existing Assembly Rooms. In 1872 the estate was bought by John Stewart, a comb manufacturer in Aberdeen whose family continued to own the estate until the house was devastated by fire in 1978. It now forms part of the Camphill Rudolph Steiner Community and is known as Beannachar.

Ardoe House

Like Banchory House, Ardoe was built on lands granted by Alexander II to the abbots of Arbroath. The estate, which extended to about 1,000 acres, was sometimes described as having a 'sunny half and a shady half'. It was bought in 1839 by Alexander Ogston, a soap manufacturer in Aberdeen who in 1853 sold the shady half known as Cotbank. He died in 1869 and his son Alexander Milne Ogston purchased the estate from his father's trustees and bought back the lands of Cotbank. In 1878 he built for his family a house in the Scottish baronial style. The architect was James Matthews and it was claimed to be a rival to Balmoral Castle. The house remained in the family until 1945 when it was sold, and then converted two years later to a hotel with fifteen rooms. It has been expanded considerably over the years. The hotel, it is claimed, has a white lady ghost who is thought to be Katherine Ogston, the wife of Alexander Milne Ogston. There is a portrait of Katherine on the main stairs and this is where her ghost has been seen. Others have reported that the ghost is a daughter of a former owner who was raped and became pregnant. She later killed herself and her child.

Kingcausie

The earliest part of the house dates to the 16th century on grounds acquired by the Irvine family of Drum from the Order of St. John in 1535. Kingcausie is one of just two mansions in Kincardineshire (the other being Arbuthnott House near Stonehaven) where the direct descendants of the original family still live there and has seen many changes over the years. The present house structure was developed by the architect David Bryce in 1853 for the 11th laird, John Irvine-Boswell, commemorated by Boswell's Monument. Bryce recorded that the house was one of his happiest compositions and it is recorded that Queen Victoria so admired its 'Abbotsford-like facade' that she asked for the royal train to be halted so that she could view it across the river. Today that view is somewhat different with the opening of the Aberdeen bypass in late 2018. The 15th laird, James Irvine-Fortescue, is remembered as the man who in 1972 arrived in Edinburgh brandishing a claymore to fight off Scottish Office plans to divide the ancient county of Kincardineshire. He won his case but had to return 21 years later when in another round of reorganisation, his beloved county was to become part of an enlarged Aberdeenshire and the position of lord lieutenant abolished. Although administratively Kincardineshire has become part of a new Aberdeenshire, the position of lord lieutenant continues.

Maryculter House

Lying along both banks of the river Dee, the lands of Culter originally included the parishes of Peterculter and Maryculter. The Knights Templar were granted lands on the south bank by William the Lion, king of Scots, in 1187. Between 1221 and 1236, Walter Bisset of Aboyne founded a preceptory for the Knights Templar on this site. The barrel-vaulted basement, which still exists, is said to have formed part of the Preceptor's Lodging. In 1312 the Knights Templar were abolished by Papal Bull and the property given to the Knights Hospitaller (the Order of St. John). When they finally abandoned Maryculter in 1548, the Menzies family of Pitfodels became the tenants and in 1618 John Menzies purchased the estate. The Menzies family are remembered by a set of initials carved on the west front of the house – W. M. and M. U. – William Menzies and Margaret Urquhart, his wife. In 1811 the estate was acquired by William Gordon of Fyvie. In 1912 Sir Cosmo Duff Gordon, who was then laird, was one of those rescued from the *Titanic*. Many stories have been told about how he became one of the survivors but afterwards he seems to have become something of a recluse at Maryculter. He died in 1931 and four years later the estate was broken up and sold. After the war the old mansion house was converted into a hotel.

Altries House

This estate, which originally formed part of the lands belonging to the Knights Templar, later became the property of John Menzies of Pitfodels. It then passed to James Gordon and was acquired by the trustees of James Kinloch in 1839. The lands not only included the parts of Maryculter, now commonly known as the estate of Altries, but also the estate of Park. They were held in favour of Alexander John Kinloch and his heirs. When the mansion house was built, soon after the lands were acquired, it was called the House of Altries. It was built on the site of an earlier house and the name is believed to have been derived from the lordship of Altrie, part of the Pitfour estate in Buchan, which James Kinloch at one time part owned. In 1887 Alexander John Kinloch paid for the stained glass windows in the local church in memory of his wife and, in 1908, the communion table was presented by his family in his memory.

Auchlunies

An early mention of Auchlonies estate recalls that Inch of Auchlunies was renamed Inch of Heathcot. It was an island in 1774, but had become joined to the north bank by 1850 and is now part of Deeside Golf Club though remaining in Maryculter parish. In 1810 the estate of Auchlonies was bought by Alexander Gordon who held it until 1834 when it was sold to Peter Duguid, a merchant in Aberdeen. The original house of Auchlunies dates from the 17th century with later additions. Peter died in 1838 and was succeeded by his son, also Peter. He resided there for many years before moving to live on the estate of Bourtie, near Oldmeldrum which he also owned. His brother William then occupied the house until his death. The house was purchased from the Duguid family in 1970 by James Nicol of Clashfarquhar, the well known Church of Scotland benefactor, and it is now subdivided into four apartments.

Heathcot

Heathcot was part of the estate of Auchlonies until 1793 when it was sold by Theophilus Ogilvie, collector of customs in Aberdeen, to Thomas Gordon. He was succeeded by his sister Lady Mary Bannerman, widow of Sir Alexander B. Bannerman who had been Professor of Medicine at Aberdeen University in the latter part of the 18th century. In 1822 John Garioch became proprietor and three years later he bought a further part of Auchlonies estate from the then proprietor Alexander Gordon on which he built a mansion house. He planted trees and improved the land and when he died his sister Margaret took over the property until her death when it was sold to James Fraser, a merchant in Aberdeen. He was succeeded as owner by Adam Mitchell, who was a very successful builder in Aberdeen with many fine buildings to his credit. He died in 1877 and the estate was acquired by Alexander Milne Ogston of Ardoe. The house had become a Hydropathic establishment in 1874 and was run very successfully by Rev. Dr. Alexander Stewart before his move to the new Deeside Hydropathic, built in 1899, about half a mile to the north of Murtle Station. Heathcot was demolished in the late 1950s to make way for a modern house.

Durris House

After Scotland had won independence from England in the 14th century, King Robert Bruce granted charters of land to his faithful followers among them Sir Robert Fraser, Lord Chamberlain of Scotland. A tower house, dating from 1620, was burnt to the ground in 1645 by the Marquis of Montrose. It was reconstructed probably in the 1660s. In 1678, after the death of Sir Peter Fraser, his daughter, who had inherited the estate, married the Earl of Peterborough and Monmouth and thus the Earl became the laird of Durris and built a mansion house dating from 1694. In 1706 their daughter married the second Duke of Gordon and thus the lands passed into the hands of that ancient family. In 1795 the estate was leased to John Innes of Leuchars who at his own expense carried out extensive improvements to the house forgetting that he was not the proprietor. In 1824 the Duke of Gordon, under an Act of Parliament, took back the property causing the ruin of John Innes. To mark his victory the Duke erected an octagonal tower not far from Park Bridge. The Duke of Gordon employed the renowned Aberdeen architect, Archibald Simpson, to add a wing to the house in 1824 and when the estate was sold in 1834 to Anthony Mactier, a wealthy East India merchant, he also employed Simpson to remodel the house. In 1871 the estate was sold to James Young, the shale oil pioneer, who was followed in 1890 by Henry Baird, the last owner of the estate. The portico shown in the photograph was demolished in 1948 and the house has now been divided into several properties.

Drum Castle

The charter granting the forest of Drum was given to William de Irwin by King Robert Bruce on 1st February 1322, (1323 in the new calendar introduced in Scotland in 1600). William was appointed one of the King's representatives in the Royal Forest of Drum, where successive kings came to hunt deer and wild boar. He was also given ownership of the Tower of Drum which probably dates from the second half of the 13th century and built for Alexander III. There was bitter enmity for many years between the Irvines and their neighbours, the Keiths, hereditary Marischals of Scotland. In 1402 at the Battle of Drumoak, the Irvines slaughtered an invading party of Keiths. The feud was only formally ended on 4th August 2002 when, at an elaborate ceremony on the banks of the River Dee, David, Chief of Clan Irvine, entered into a peace treaty with Michael, Earl of Kintore, Chief of the Keith Clan. There are many instances of the fighting talent of the Irvines; Sir Alexander Irvine had led his Clan at the battle of Harlaw and during the 17th and 18th centuries the Irvines remained fiercely Royalist and Jacobite. The 17th laird paid the price when he fought at Culloden, resulting in the family losing some of the lands of Drum. An elegant Jacobean mansion was added on to the old tower in 1619 and substantially remodelled for the family by David and John Bryce between 1875 and 1882. On the death, in 1975, of the 24th laird, Henry Quentin Forbes Irvine, the property was acquired by the National Trust for Scotland.

Drum Castle, Deeside.

Drum Lodge, Deeside.

Park House, Deeside.

East Lodge, Park, Deeside

Park

When King Robert Bruce granted part of the Royal Forest of Drum to the Irvine family in 1323, he reserved for himself the royal hunting lands of Park. His grandson, Robert II granted the whole of the Park to the Irvines in 1389 and it remained in their possession until 1737. Thereafter it had several owners until 1821 when it was acquired by William Moir, a wealthy Aberdeen businessman. He employed architect Archibald Simpson to build a grand house in the then very fashionable Neo Greek style. The house cannot be seen from the North Deeside Road and is best viewed from across the river. In 1839 Alexander John Low became proprietor under rather unusual circumstances. James Kinloch, a native of Kincardineshire, who had made his fortune in India, died a bachelor and left a substantial sum of money to the family of his sister, a Mrs. Low, on the understanding that it would be invested in the purchase of land in Scotland and that his heir would assume the name of Kinloch. Hence Alexander Low became a Kinloch. In 1888 the estate was purchased from Mr Kinloch's trustees by Andrew Penny, a silver and copper mine owner of Oruro, Bolivia. He was a native of the parish of Birse and intended to make the house his home, but en route for Scotland he died. After the First World War, Park House was bought by Sir Robert Williams, who had acted as advisor and sometime partner to Cecil Rhodes, in the early pioneering days of South Africa. Williams was a gifted and entrepreneurial Scottish mining engineer and railroad developer who discovered the vast copper deposits in Katanga Province (now part of the Democratic Republic of Congo) and Northern Rhodesia (now Zambia).

Crathes Castle

Crathes is the traditional home of the Burnett family, lairds of Leys. King Robert Bruce granted the lands to Alexander de Burnard by a charter dated 28th March 1323. Originally the family lived just north of Banchory on what is known as a crannog (a fortress built of timbers on an island they constructed in the middle of a bog). Two centuries later, in 1553, Alexander Burnett and his wife Janet Hamilton commissioned a new home for the family. On the wall above the old yett gate, the original entry to the castle, are two coats of arms – the first dated 1553 is their coat of arms and the other that of their great-grandson Alexander and his wife Katherine Gordon dated 1596 when the castle was heightened to its present form by the Bell family, architects from Midmar. The castle is recognised as a fine example of Scottish Renaissance. The internal rooms of the castle are well preserved and the plaster and painted ceilings are particularly fine. In the Great Hall hangs the famous jewelled ivory hunting horn traditionally said to have been given by King Robert Bruce to Alexander de Burnard. The castle gardens are justly renowned with a splendid collection of British and foreign shrubs and plants, and the massive yew hedges which date from 1702. The castle was given to the National Trust for Scotland in 1951 by the 13th baronet Sir James Burnett. The three storey Queen Anne wing of the castle, added in the early 18th century, was burnt to a shell in 1966. It has now been rebuilt but has been greatly reduced in size.

Balnacraig

Sir Robert Burnett of Leys owned the lands of Corsee and in a plan of 1877 John Gray Chalmers is indicated as the feuar of the ground on which he built his house, Balnacraig, in Banchory. He was the last surviving great grandson of James Chalmers, the founder of the *Aberdeen Journal*. The house was built in 1887 of local granite from Hill of Fare. He died in 1890 and left £10,000 in his will to invest in the *Journal*'s future. More than half of the legacy was used to buy premises in Broad Street, remembered by many, which was the home of the *Aberdeen Journal* until 1970. By 1897 the house was the home of Rev. Charles Dunn who had been minister of Birse since 1864. After his death in 1908 his widow gifted the bell which graced the Lady Burnett school in Banchory, later the Burgh buildings. Corsee Road still has many fine granite houses dating from the late 19th century. Among them are Druimdarroch, the home of Dr. David Lawson, the founder of the Nordrach-on-Dee Sanatorium in 1900, now a ruin after a fire in 2016; Wynndun the home of John Petrie Bisset, Provost of Banchory from 1893-1903; Cairntoigh the home of George Milne Cook a ship-owner in Aberdeen and Lynwood owned by Alexander Hossack a retired Aberdeen fruit merchant.

Raemoir House

Behind Raemoir House is the old Ha' Hoose (Hall House). The stone over the entrance indicates it was constructed circa 1715 for the Hogg Family. The Hoggs succeeded to the estate when Margaret Skene, the daughter of Robert Skene of Raemoir married James Hogg. Raemoir House was built in front of the old house and George Robertson writing in 1807 describes it as 'a plain modern house situated amidst a few straggling trees, on the south side of the Hill of Fare'. John Smith was the architect in 1817 who added the west wing for William Innes, a merchant from London. William set about improving the estate and in 1844 added the entrance porch using the same architect and his son William Smith. The estate was purchased in 1927 by Viscount and Lady Cowdray, who commissioned alterations to the building, principally the addition of the east wing. The architect on this occasion was William Kelly. In 1943 the house became a hotel leased from the Cowdray family of Dunecht. This hotel was a place of peace and tranquillity for those wanting to escape for a few days from London in the later days of Second World War. It was at one point referred to as 'The Claridges of the North' a reference to the famous hotel in London's Mayfair. It is now under corporate ownership and no longer a hotel.

Cairnton (old house)

Cairnton, west of Banchory, was part of the lands belonging to the Burnetts of Crathes and was rented from 1913 until 1934 by Arthur Wood, who was passionate about salmon fishing. The original house had modest accommodation but he demolished it and built a new house which opened for the start of the 1921 fishing season. Wood had a great knowledge of salmon fishing and was an expert fisherman. James Burnett of Leys in his book *Crannog to Castle* records that in the fishing records for 1915 Wood caught 265 salmon at Cairnton including 121 during the last 13 days. When he died in 1934 Cairnton reverted to Crathes Estates and later was rented by Ivan Cobbold who had married Lady Blanche Cavendish, the daughter of the 9th Duke of Devonshire.

Cairnton (new house)

His brother-in-law was Harold Macmillan. In April 1944, just weeks before D-Day, General Eisenhower along with General Walter Bedell Smith, his chief of staff, travelled to Banchory on Ike's special train to fish at Cairnton as guests of Cobbold. On Friday 14th April Bedell Smith caught two – a 7½ pound salmon using a sweep fly and an 8 pound salmon using a silver grey fly on the Grey Mare Pool but no mention of Eisenhower. He must have had an unsuccessful day on the river! Ivan Cobbold tragically was killed just weeks later. Cairnton was sold in 1947 by Sir James Burnett to William Mitchell and it remained in his family until 2006 when it was sold to its present owner.

Woodend House

Woodend House, lying a few miles west of Banchory, dates from the 17th century and is sited on one of the most beautiful stretches of the River Dee with its excellent fishing beats. It was originally part of the Crathes Estate and was sold in 1946. The Dee rises at the Wells of Dee near the summit of Braeriach amongst the Grampian Mountains at a height of over 4,000 feet and follows a course of over 85 miles to the North Sea at Aberdeen – initially dropping 2,000 feet into Glen Dee and becoming the fastest flowing river in Scotland. The river provides the angler with some of the best salmon beats in Scotland. The fishing season now commences on the 1st February and finishes on 15th October each year. The Dee is very much a fly-fishing river with beautiful boulder-strewn attractive clear water pools that ebb and flow throughout its entire length. In 1994 the River Dee management made the river 100% 'catch and release'. This initiative was as an attempt to increase salmon stocks but so far there has been little few sign of improvement.

Inchmarlo House

Inchmarlo House stands about a mile west of Banchory. In the 17th century the lands were acquired by the Douglas family who also were lairds of nearby Tilquhillie. In the late 18th century a two storey house was built for John Douglas of Tilquhillie. In 1812 the estate passed into the hands of Walter Davidson, a London banker, and in 1823 the house was remodelled by the architect John Smith. The estate was sold in 1838 to Duncan Davidson (no relation of Walter Davidson). His son Patrick, in 1850, commissioned the architects John and William Smith to add a third storey with flat roof and balustrade parapet to the house. Patrick objected to the suggested route of the extended railway line to Aboyne being built between the house and the river and sold land east of the Glassel Road to the Deeside Railway Company to allow for an alternative route via Glassel and Lumphanan. The Davidsons were responsible for the planting of the magnificent woodlands. Before the railway line was built and then extended beyond Banchory, Queen Victoria on her way to Balmoral would order her coach to be driven through the estate to appreciate its beauty. The estate was acquired in 1983 by Skene Enterprises and after major renovation it was opened in 1987 as a nursing home and retirement complex.

West Lodge, Inchmarlo, Banchory.

Inchmarlo Cottage

Inchmarlo Cottage, built in 1880, is situated at the west end of Banchory Golf Course. It was originally the home of Patrick Davidson's widow and later that of their youngest son, George Louis Outram Davidson, born in 1858. He was, as a young boy, fascinated by flight and was known locally as 'Fleein Geordie fae Inchmarlo!' He was to continue this interest for most of his life and set up a workshop in the cottage experimenting initially with gliders, and then a powered machine. In 1898 he made what he called a gyrocopter with flapping wings, which actually became airborne, at least for a few yards, much to the delight of the large crowd who had gathered to watch. He died in 1939 and his gravestone records that he was a founder member of the Royal Aeronautical Society.

Banchory Lodge

William Burnett was born in 1762 and was the youngest son of Sir Thomas Burnett of Leys, the 6th baronet. He had acquired Arbeadie, on the north side of the river Dee, from his eldest brother Sir Robert Burnett, the 7th baronet. Thus was established Banchory Lodge Estate. In the early 1800s William had the old Coble Heugh Inn incorporated into a new mansion house which was renamed Banchory Lodge. So the quaint little hostelry was transformed into a stately house in the dignified style of the period and around it was created extensive and beautiful grounds which obliterated all traces of the old Deeside road. William died unmarried in 1839 and three years later the Scolty Tower was built in his memory by his friends and tenants. The estate then passed to his great nephew William Burnett Ramsay. When he died in 1865 he was remembered by a handsome granite fountain still to be seen close to one of the then entrances to the estate on Station Road. He was succeeded first by his son Thomas Burnett Ramsay and then in 1901 by one of Thomas's sisters, Miss Katharine Burnett Ramsay who at the time was living with the another surviving sister, Anne, at Riverstone, sometimes written as Riverston, a house on the estate, across the river from Banchory Lodge. Anne married Walter Guy Bentinck and the last proprietor of Banchory Lodge was their son Thomas Bentinck. In 1936 Banchory Lodge was sold and became a hotel.

Riverstone House

The earliest part of Riverstone House was a 17th century U-plan house with east and west wings and a cross passage, all enclosing a courtyard open to the north. This plan essentially survived until major development during the 19th century when the orientation was reversed to become a bay fronted house facing south to the River Feugh. The first floor position of the 19th century drawing room in the east wing suggested the position of a 17th century hall. There was some evidence that the cellar below the east wing was originally vaulted. The house was part of the Banchory Lodge estate until 1949 when, except for the hotel, it was sold. Thereafter the house had various owners but in 2017 it suffered major internal damage resulting in it being demolished in 2019.

Tilquhillie Castle

Tilquhillie Castle, (pronounced *Tilwhillie*) lies two miles south of Banchory. The lands originally belonged to the Abbey of Arbroath but in the 16th century, in the aftermath of the Reformation, the first named owner was Walter Ogston whose daughter and heiress Janet Ogston married David Douglas in 1479. The castle was built by his grandson John in 1576 as a Z-plan fortified house and commanded the Mounth route to the crossing of the Dee at Banchory. A later generation of castle owners lived in troubled times. The then laird John Douglas was killed in battle in 1632 and the estate suffered badly with the castle besieged and then garrisoned by the Covenanters. The lands were now heavily in debt, not helped by the purchase of Inchmarlo in around 1664 by James Douglas. His son returned from a career as a merchant in the East Indies to clear the debts. In 1812 Tilquhillie estate was sold on the death of the then laird John Douglas to Henry Lumsden of Pitcaple but was bought back in 1865 by his son, also named John, who had made a substantial fortune in the manufacturing business in the Tyrol. The castle by this time had been more or less been abandoned in favour of the more comfortable Invery House. For many years the castle was lived in by the tenant of the farm, which surrounds the castle, and was left unoccupied in 1948. With new owners the old castle has now been very tastefully restored.

Blackhall Castle

The Blackhall Estate was originally the home of the ancient family of Russell. The last of the male line of the Russells of Blackhall was drowned on the Dee in 1827 and his sister, Frances, who had married Archibald Farquharson of Finzean succeeded to the estate. The laird made substantial alterations to the castle but this, together with his propensity for gambling and enjoying the social life, ruined him financially and the estate was sold first to Colonel John Campbell and later to James T. Hay. He replaced the old castle in 1884 with a building having many similarities to Balmoral Castle.

The estate suffered serious deforestation in both World Wars. During the Second World War, the castle housed St. Margaret's School for Girls from Aberdeen. The castle was demolished in 1946 and some of its fine granite blocks were used to repair bomb damage to the Houses of Parliament in London. The original gateway to the estate remains but without the figure of the goat and below the family motto, *Che sara sara* – what will be will be. The goat and the stone with the family motto have been located in separate places in Banchory. Perhaps one day they might be together again but probably not in the original position on top of the gateway.

Feugh Lodge

In 1870 John Douglas, who had made Invery his home, died and was succeeded by his son John Sholto Douglas. He was killed by a fall from a precipice in the Tyrol and his eldest son, also John, became the new laird when he came of age in 1886. He had a son named after his grandfather born in 1904. With Invery sold and their ancestral home Tilquhillie Castle derelict, Feugh Lodge became the family home after the death of his father in 1925. Sholto Douglas had a most distinguished army service. The house is just west of the Feugh Bridge. Jane Geddes in her book on the architecture of the Mearns and Deeside describes the house as 'a picturesque Gothic agglomeration perched on a cliff edge'. The house has a private pedestrian bridge from the north bank to the south bank of the Feugh.

Invery House

The lands of Invery had come into the ownership of the Douglas family at the same time as they acquired Tilquhillie. Around the 1680s the first house was built, later improved on by Mr. Rose. By 1795 it was beginning to take on its present appearance when Mr. Leith added to the house. In around 1800 Invery belonged to James Skene of Rubislaw, a close friend of Sir Walter Scott who was a frequent visitor to Invery. Scott wrote parts of *Marmion* while at the house and James, who was an artist, illustrated the first edition of the book. In 1816 Skene moved to Edinburgh and among his notable achievements was his design for Princes Street Gardens. By this time the estate, along with Tilquhillie, had been sold but both were bought back in 1865 by the wealthy John Douglas who made it his home. In 1903 Invery House and its policies were bought by the Kerr family of Paisley who again made changes to the appearance of the house. In 1986 it was bought by the Spence family and it became the Invery House Hotel, with the bedrooms all named after novels written by Sir Walter Scott. In 1994 it was sold and once again it is a family home.

Glendye Lodge

Glendye Lodge, dating from 1779, was built as a shooting lodge for the Carnegie family of Southesk. It is situated close to the Cairn O Mounth road on an area of steeply wooded ground beside the Bridge of Dye, which dates from around 1680. The lodge was sold in 1856 to the Gladstones of Fasque and it remains part of the Fasque and Glen Dye estate. The road used to be the main route south from Royal Deeside and follows the line of a military road built by General George Wade in the 1700s. He formalised a route that had been used by, among many others, the English army in 1296, Macbeth on his way to defeat at the Battle of Lumphanan in 1057, and the Roman army of Julius Agricola in AD 84. The origin of the name of the road is *Mounth* – the Scots word for mountain – and the Cairn, dating from prehistoric times, refers possibly to the pile of rocks at the summit of the road from Strachan to Fettercairn.

Finzean House

The Farquharsons can trace their ancestry back to the late 14th century but it was not until 1609 that Robert Farquharson bought the lands of Finzean (pronounced *Fing-an*, from the Gaelic meaning 'fair place'). 'Their descendants', Sir Angus Farquharson wrote in 2009, 'have survived war, civil strife, economic disaster and bankruptcy, maintaining their link with Finzean, probably because of a deep attachment to a most beautiful valley and a much loved home'. The original mansion was built in 1689 and in 1707 Queen Anne granted Robert Farquharson, the 4th laird, a charter ensuring his independence from any feudal superior except the Crown. In 1747 Frances Farquharson, his son, added the south front. Considerable alterations were again made to the house in 1790 and about 1860 the three gables and entrance door were added. The Right Hon. Dr. Robert Farquharson, the 11th laird, was for 26 years the Member of Parliament for West Aberdeenshire and in 1918 he was succeeded as laird by his brother Joseph Farquharson, R.A. He gained great fame as a landscape painter and is particularly remembered for his local scenes, many of which included sheep and snow. In 1954 a disastrous fire destroyed part of the property but the present house retains the traditional frontage.

Forest of Birse Castle

The Bishops of Aberdeen sold off their properties in Birse between 1549 and 1620, and granted to the new landowners (and their tenants) the common right to use the forest for timber, peat and grazing. William Gordon of Cluny feued the Forest of Birse in 1585 and in 1610 he enclosed the best part of the common grazing, brought in tenant farmers, and built a castle. After falling into debt, the Gordons sold the forest to William Douglas of Glenbervie in 1636 and in 1640 the other landowners in Birse burnt down the castle in order to re-establish their common rights. In 1666 the forest was sold to the Earl of Aboyne and in 1897 Joseph Robert Heaven bought the estate and rebuilt Birse Castle in 1905. On his death in 1911 the Forest of Birse was bought by Weetman Pearson, 1st Viscount Cowdray and became part of his Dunecht estate. In 1930 the castle was substantially extended for Annie Pearson, Viscountess Cowdray by Dr. William Kelly.

Balfour House

The Balfour estate was sold to the Marquis of Huntly by the executors of Alexander Farquharson, the last laird who died in 1791. In 1840 the Aberdeen advocate, Francis J Cochran bought Balfour from the Marquis. It is interesting to note that not only was he related through his mother to the Marquis, but his wife Elizabeth was the great granddaughter of the last Farquharson. Five years later he built the house which at the time was described as 'a good mansion house built in the modern style of architecture'. Jane Geddes in her *Deeside and Mearns Guide* is less complimentary 'the garden front has a rhythm of five gables while the asymmetrical entrance front is rather straggling'. To this day Balfour has been the home of the Cochran family.

Bogieshiel Lodge

Bogieshiel Lodge, formerly Upper Bogieshiel, is situated on a hillside overlooking much of the Ballogie estate. The ancient name of the estate was Tillysnaught, and in 1650 belonged to a branch of the Roses of Kilravock. It passed afterwards to a Forbes, then the Innes and Farquharson families, before being sold to James Dyce Nicol, MP for Kincardineshire from 1865-72. The lodge, which dates from the 18th century, was used as the priest's house after the Catholic community had moved from Deecastle, near Aboyne, in 1815. Originally the house was traditional in style but the later addition of the bowed bay to the south is unusual on the estate.

Ballogie House

In 1850 Ballogie Estate, which includes the land south of the Bridge of Potarch, was bought by James Dyce Nicol and a few years later a house designed by James Matthews was built on the site of an earlier 18th century house. Writing in 1865 Robert Dinnie, a noted stonemason and historian, thought little of the design stating that 'it presented nothing particularly interesting in an architectural point of view'. Robert was the father of Donald Dinnie whose birthplace was at Balnacraig on the Ballogie estate. His sporting career began at the age of 16 and spanned over 50 years. Donald, like his father Robert, was a stonemason. While helping his father in around 1860 repair the Bridge at Potarch, Donald lifted two enormous stones, one weighing 340 pounds and the other 435 pounds and carried them across the bridge a distance of five yards. The stones were being used as anchors at either side of the wooden structure while the work was being carried out. Normally the stones would have been outside the entrance to the 18th century Potarch Inn, where travellers on horseback used the rings on the top to tether their horses. Ballogie House was replaced by a more compact dwelling for Col. John Nicol in 1983. The estate continues to be owned by the family.

Glassel House

In *The Agricultural Survey of Kincardineshire* published in 1807, Glassel House, which is north west of Banchory, is described as 'a mansion, having pretty extensive and laid out gardens, with a hot-house and some beautiful shrubbery'. The house had been built in the mid 1700s for the Baxters of Aberdeen who traded with Russia. They had worked hard on improving the ground, stones were removed and were used to fill drains, make roads and also build walls around the fields. Some of these walls were up to 12-16 feet in thickness and were known as 'consumption dykes'. In 1823 the house and grounds came into the ownership of the Mitchell family from Yorkshire, but sadly they neglected it until the late 1800s when alterations began to be made. An east wing was added in 1902 in what has been termed 'half-hearted Neo Romanesque style' and a west wing in 1912 in Baronial style. When Arthur H. Wood, the eminent fisherman, bought the house in 1915 he instructed the architect George Bennett Mitchell to make changes leaving it more like a like a suburban villa. Outside, however, the gardens received great attention; a rock garden was built in the ground between the house and the old bridge and what was known as a bee well was constructed. Over the years these features became neglected but the present owners have had them restored.

Craigmyle

The fine old Ha' House of Craigmyle which stood about two miles west of Glassel was demolished in 1960. It was an excellent example of late 17th century architecture and stood on the lower slopes of the Hill of Fare facing south-west. It was built in 1696 by Isabel Burnett of Craigmyle and her husband John Farquharson of Invercauld. For a few years prior to 1887 there was a private platform on the Deeside railway line for the use of the residents of the house and visitors. In 1902 the house was added to by the then owner R. P. Robertson-Glasgow from designs by Sir Robert Lorimer. In 1911 the estate was purchased by Thomas Shaw, the distinguished law lord who was created in 1929 1st Baron Craigmyle. In 1956 the ancient barony of Craigmyle was broken up and four years later the house was demolished and replaced by a bungalow which retains the triple arch loggia and granite front door piece of the 1902 house. A short distance from the original house was a grand old tree known locally as the 'Darnley Ash' though it is extremely unlikely that Lord Darnley planted it. Indeed the tale that Lord Darnley visited Craigmyle after the Battle of Corrichie, fought nearby on the Hill of Fare in 1562, is certainly without foundation as he was in England at the time. The tree was cut down in 1960.

The Firs

The development of Torphins following the arrival in 1859 of the railway was dramatic. It encouraged the building of weekend country houses, one of them being The Firs. It was designed by architect Alexander Ellis in 1890 to his own design for his own use and built by his brother-in-law, John Morgan, The style was influenced by houses Morgan had seen in Toronto and Montreal. In his long and varied career, he was responsible for the design of a number of notable buildings, including the original Joint Station, the frontage to Marischal College, the Central Library and the Northern Insurance Building (known locally as the Monkey House). They had known one another from at least 1863 when Morgan had been involved in the building of Corse House which Ellis had designed. Ellis had to retire in 1896 through illness. He made a voyage to Australia in the spring of 1897 in the hope of a cure and recovered sufficiently to design, in 1898, a house in what was once known as Glenburnie Road, Rubislaw Den, close to where Glenburnie Distillery once stood. He spent the remaining twenty years of his life divided between his two houses. In 1920 his widow sold it to Alexander James Webster, a timber merchant and William Webster, an accountant, both of Peterhead.

Pitmurchie House

Pitmurchie House has a commanding view of Torphins and is set within beautiful grounds with lovely views of the countryside. In the *Old Statistical Account* mention is made of a font stone being at the manse of Lumphanan. In 1829 the daughter of the writer of that account, the Rev. William Shand, removed the basin to Pitmurchie on her marriage to Harry Lamont of Pitmurchie. There it served as a watering trough for some years until it was restored once again to the manse. The original house dates from prior to 1842 when the landowner is listed as Mrs. Lamont, but in 1886 the architects Matthews & Mackenzie reconstructed the house adding bow fronted wings for their client H.J. Barlow, an Aberdeen lawyer. Sometime before the First World War, Haddon Anderson Bower of Bower & Florence, granite merchants in Aberdeen, wanted to pursue his other interests in the city's businesses. He bought the estate of Pitmurchie and became greatly respected for his knowledge of affairs connected with farm and land management, and for his promotion of the recycling of by-products from the distilling industry for agricultural use as feeding cake for animals, to prevent the polluting of rivers. Today it is a care home.

Learney

The Learney Estate has been in the ownership of the Innes family for over 200 years. Learney was originally part of the Durward barony of O'Neil and then passed though the Irvines of Drum and the Forbeses of Craigievar to the Brebner family in 1747. William Brebner built the old Ha' House in 1750 and was succeeded by his son Alexander. Jane, his eldest daughter, married William Innes. The central block was destroyed by fire in 1837 and rebuilt the following year, but the final chapter in the evolution of the house was the work of Col. Thomas Innes second son of Jane and William. He redesigned the two wings in the late 1860s. Col. Innes recognised the potential of the coming of the railway to Torphins in 1859 and welcomed its construction over his land. At that time Torphins consisted of a few thatched cottages and an old inn but its development after the extension of the Deeside railway was dramatic. Col. Innes was regarded as the founder of modern Torphins and died aged 98 in 1912. His descendants have given further distinction to the family by providing two Lord Lyons, Kings of Arms in recent years.